THE AMAZING UNIVERSE

*Translated from the Italian
by Maureen Spurgeon*

ENGLAND

© 2001 Istituto Geografico De Agostini, Novara
© 2003 Brown Watson, English edition
Reprinted 2003

WHAT IS A STAR?

The stars that we see shining in the sky at night are spheres of very hot gas which give off a strong light. For a star to shine, it has to reach a temperature of around 10 million degrees Centigrade! The colour of a star depends on its size and its temperature. The largest are also the hottest, and shine with a blue light. Some smaller stars shine with a white light, some yellow, others orange or pink. The different ways in which they shine also depends on their distance from Earth. The closer the star, the more clearly we see its light. Smaller stars have an average diameter of a few thousand kilometres. The diameter of the largest stars can reach up to three billion kilometres!

BILLIONS OF STARS

Scientists estimate that there are 200 billion, billion stars. About 3000 can be seen with the naked eye in each hemisphere of the Earth. Seen from our planet, the stars all seem to be at the same distance. In fact, they are at many different distances.

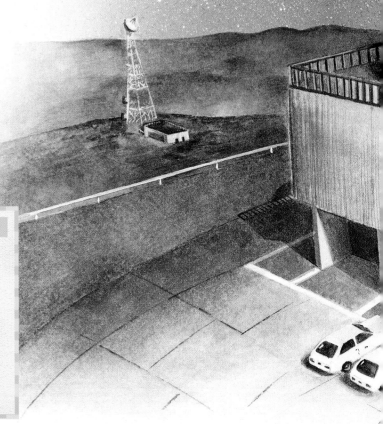

• HOW WHY WHEN •

What is a Light Year?

The unit of measurement used to calculate enormous distances in space is the Light Year – that is, the distance which light travels in one year. One Light Year is equal to 9460 billion kilometres. Try to work out the diameter of the Milky Way (100,000 Light Years) in kilometres, and you will get a number which you would not be able to pronounce!

FACTS·AND·FIGURES

- The star nearest to us, excluding the Sun, is Proxima Centurai, which is 4.3 Light Years from Earth.
- The largest star is the supergiant Betelgeuse which is 520 Light Years from us. Its diameter is about 400 times greater than that of the Sun.
- The star which looks brightest from Earth is Sirius – its name means 'shining'. It is 8.6 Light Years from our planet.

NEBULAE

Nebulae are clouds of dust and gas in which there may be the origins of stars. Sometimes, they are the remains of 'dying' stars. Some nebulae shine due to the presence of very hot stars. Others are dark and quite dense.

HOW IS A STAR BORN?

The life of a star begins at the heart of a nebula. Together, gas and dust form a nucleus which is always very dense and hot. When the temperature reaches about 10 million degrees Centigrade, the nucleus ignites and the star begins to shine, burning hydrogen, which is one of its basic elements, for billions of years.

A star of great dimensions (supergiant) burns very quickly and in the end explodes. From this explosion there forms a supernova.

A star of medium dimensions, for example a 'yellow dwarf' like our Sun, once it exhausts the hydrogen, becomes bigger and brighter, changing into a 'red giant'.

Gradually, its nucleus shrinks again, slowly becoming cooler and heavier. Now the golden star is a 'white dwarf' which will gradually cool down until it is extinguished altogether.

WHAT IS A GALAXY?

A galaxy is a huge mass of stars, gas and dust, all kept together by the force of gravity, and rotating around a central point. In the Universe there are billions of galaxies. A galaxy can comprise between one billion to 100,000 billion stars. There are galaxies of different forms and sizes. The elliptic (oval) galaxy has old stars and is generally large and bright. Spiral galaxies have 'long' arms spiralling out from a central nucleus. Those 'arms' contain mainly new stars, and are where new stars may begin. Irregular galaxies do not have an exact formation. They are usually small and rich in gas and dust.

MASSES AND MASSES OF GALAXIES

Galaxies tend to group together, forming masses of a hundred or a thousand galaxies. Sometimes, these can develop into super-clusters, comprising hundreds of masses!

● HOW WHY WHAT WHEN ●

What is a Black Hole?

The explosion of a big star can generate a Black Hole – that is, a heavenly body in which the force of gravity is so strong that it does not allow anything to escape, not even light. That is why a Black Hole cannot be seen, not even with the most powerful telescope.

BARRED SPIRALS

Some spiral galaxies are cut through with a straight bar of stars at the centre with spiral 'arms' branching off at the end. These galaxies are called 'barred spirals'.

QUASARS

All Quasars (quasi-stellar object) are millions of light years away from Earth. A Quasar looks like a star, but it is widely believed that it is actually the nucleus of a galaxy, with a black hole at the centre.

- The Milky Way, like other galaxies, is rotating slowly around, like a huge ring. It takes 230 million years to make a complete circuit.
- The nearest galaxies to us are the Small Magellanic Cloud and the Large Magellanic Cloud. Smaller than the Milky Way, these are only visible to the naked eye in southern (austral) skies.
- The furthest galaxy visible with the naked eye is Andromeda. Its light takes more than two million years to reach Earth. So, we see it as it was two million years ago.
- The diameter of the Milky Way is about 100,000 Light Years.

WHAT IS THE MILKY WAY?

The Milky Way is our galaxy. It gets its name because in the starry sky, it appears to the naked eye as a milky-white trail. It is a spiral galaxy, with the Sun and other planets in one of its 'arms', that of Orion, which is 33000 Light Years from the centre.

All that we see in the sky with the naked eye belongs to our galaxy, with the exception of three patches which, in fact, are other galaxies.

WHAT ARE COMETS?

Comets are spheres of frozen gases and dust. They travel around the Sun on very long orbits. As it nears the Sun, the heat evaporates the comet's surface and this produces a shining globe of gas and dust around the nucleus and trail of vapour. This trail is pushed away from the Sun by Solar Winds to form the tail of the comet. A comet's tail can be up to hundreds of millions of kilometres long and always goes in the opposite direction to the Sun. The trail and the tail of a comet are visible because both spread the solar light. Slowly, slowly, as the comet draws further away from the Sun, the tail gets shorter until it disappears altogether.

• HOW WHY WHAT WHEN •

When was a Comet last seen?

The larger the comet, the longer its orbit, which can take thousands or millions of years.
Therefore, its appearance is always a big event.
Halley's Comet is the only one which returns every 76 years. Its last sighting was in 1986.

WHAT ARE FALLING STARS?

Falling stars are actually small pieces of rock and metal from a comet. When these enter our atmosphere at high speed, they change into shining, bright vapour and light up the sky with a shining trail.

DOUBLE TAIL

The tail of a comet is actually two tails – one, straight and gaseous, and the other, wide and curved, made of dust particles.

- The largest meteorite was found in 1920 in Africa. It weighed about 60 tonnes and measured 2.7 x 2.4 metres.
- The most spectacular crater made by a meteorite is the Devil's Canyon Meteor Crater in Arizona, USA. This has a diameter of more than 1200 metres and is 183 deep. It is thought that this crater was made about 50,000 years ago.

THE SUN CONSUMES COMETS

As they pass near the Sun, a comet loses one centimetre from its external layer per day. So, in time a comet is destined to be consumed completely.

The scientific name for a falling star is a meteor. In August the Earth passes through a trail of meteors, and many 'falling stars' often appear in the night sky at that time. Some of the larger meteors do not disintegrate in the atmosphere, but fall to Earth. These are called meteorites and can be large enough to make enormous craters in the Earth's surface.

WHAT IS THE SUN?

The Sun is a star, an enormous globe of shining gas. At the centre, at a temperature of 15 million degrees Centigrade, are nuclear reactors capable of releasing an enormous quantity of energy. Only the tiniest, smallest part of this energy reaches Earth and this energy is essential to give life to our planet. The Sun is the centre of a system of planets of which Earth is a part. It is about 150 million kilometres away from us. To have some idea of how large the Sun is, imagine a huge container which could hold one million and a half planets as big as the Earth.

THE AGE OF THE SUN

Compared to the age of other stars, the Sun is not all that old. It is a 'yellow dwarf', which came into existence about 5 billion years ago. It will shine for another 5 billion years.

• HOW WHY WHAT WHEN •

What is the speed of light?

Light travels at a speed of 300,000km per second. Even at the distance between the Sun and the Earth at around 150 million kilometres, light takes 8.5 minutes to reach our planet.

PROTECTION FROM THE SUN

The atmosphere is like a thick blanket of gases which surrounds the Earth. It protects our planet from the Sun's harmful radiation, whilst keeping in enough heat to prevent the Earth from freezing over.

Q·U·I·Z

1) *How many times larger is the diameter of the Sun to the diameter of the Earth?*

❑ 50   ❑ 109   ❑ 240

2) *What type of heavenly body is the Sun?*

❑ liquid   ❑ gaseous   ❑ solid

3) *From the time it began life, the Sun has journeyed around the galaxies how many times?*

❑ 15 times   ❑ 20 times   ❑ 23 times

Answers
1) 109   2) gaseous   3) 23 times

WHY DOES THE SUN RISE AT DAWN?

The Sun does not actually rise at dawn. It is the Earth which moves, spinning on its own axis whilst at the same time it is in orbit around the Sun.

WHAT IS THERE AT THE CENTRE OF THE SUN?

Prominence

Like every star at the middle phase of its life, the Sun shines because it is burning the hydrogen contained in its nucleus and which it transforms into another gas, helium. The light and the colour which result from this reaction comes from the nucleus and spreads towards the external part, going through different layers of the Sun until it reaches its Photosphere or visible surface (after 200,000 years!) From here, the light and heat spreads at great speed into the space surrounding it.

Photosphere

Nucleus

THE ROTATION OF THE SUN

The Sun rotates on its own, but, because it is a gaseous body, it does not have a regular speed. It spins round its equator every 25 Earth days, 31 Earth days at its Poles.

● HOW WHY WHAT WHEN ●

Is it possible to explore the Sun?

The temperature of the Sun, which, even on the surface, is about 6000°C makes it impossible for anyone to explore it on site. From Earth, we can only see the Photosphere.
From 1996 the Space Probe Soho has been positioned between the Earth and the Sun, observing the Sun 24 hours a day. It has sent back to Earth a great deal of data about the Sun's activity.

CYCLE OF ACTIVITY

Corona

Chromosphere

Activity on the Sun, such as prominences and sunspots, waxes and wanes during the 'Solar Cycle'. Activity reaches a peak every 11 years, when at maximum, the number of sunspots increase.

Sunspots

The temperature of the Sun

• Nucleus: 15,000,000°C.
The part of the Sun in which hydrogen is transformed into helium generates light and heat.
• The Chromosphere: between 8000 and 20,000°C.
Gaseous, red-hot layer which constitutes the solar atmosphere.
• Photosphere: 5700°C. Luminous surface.
• Corona: 1,000,000°C. The most external zone of the Sun, visible during a Solar Eclipse. It extends for millions of kilometres and the Solar Wind forms from its particles.
• Sunspots. 4500°C. Dark zone of the Photosphere and where the temperature is lower.
• Prominence: more than 10,000°C.
A gas jet which rises for thousands of kilometres.

CONVECTIVE AND RADIATIVE ZONES

The Convective Zone is the layer of the Sun in which bubbles of shining gas transmit energy to the outside. The Radiative Zone is the area where energy passes from the nucleus to the outer layer.

WHAT IS THE SOLAR WIND?

The Corona (outer atmosphere) of the Sun releases a flow of tiny particles which travel through space at speeds of hundreds of kilometres per second in the form of the Solar Wind, which expands into the Solar System.

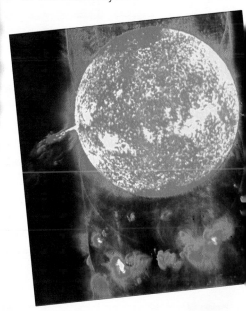

WHAT IS THE SOLAR SYSTEM?

The Sun, with its powerful force of attraction, keeps in orbit around itself 9 planets, including the Earth, 68 listed satellites, countless asteroids, meteors and comets, and a great quantity of dust and gas. Planets are spherical bodies, small and cold. They shine because they reflect the light from the star around which they orbit. Other heavenly bodies called satellites often orbit around planets. There is no life on satellites. Asteroids are minor planets, small and rocky. They orbit around the Sun between Mars and Jupiter, forming a flattened ring with a diameter of 12 billions of kilometres.

● HOW WHY WHAT WHEN ●

When did the Universe begin?

According to the most popular theory, the Universe began with a big explosion, the Big Bang, which happened 15 billion years ago. From this began the expansion of the Universe. This expansion continues today, shown by the progressive moving away of galaxies, one from another. The matter from the Big Bang became cooler, little by little, and from this originated the planets, the stars and the galaxies.

THE DIRECTION OF ROTATION
Planets orbit around the Sun, whilst at the same time rotating on their own axis. These rotations are mostly anti-clockwise; only the planet Venus rotates in a clockwise direction.

THINGS·TO·DO

With a light-coloured felt-tipped pen, draw some galaxies of different shapes on a flat blue or black balloon. As you inflate the balloon, you will see, little by little, the galaxies gradually spreading away from each other, as the surface of the balloon expands. Much the same thing happens in the Universe. This is just one model used by scientists to demonstrate the expansion of the Universe.

HOW WAS THE SOLAR SYSTEM BORN?

At least 5 billion years ago, a cloud of gas and dust began to squeeze together, spinning rather like a whirlwind. At the centre of this whirlwind the gas began to thicken, forming a star, the Sun. Away from the centre, the particles continued to spin and to collect together, forming clusters which became bigger and bigger. These were the planets, which then began to orbit around the Sun. From the smaller fragments began the asteroid belt, which also began to orbit around the Sun.

THE SHAPE OF ORBITS

In their journeys around the Sun, planets follow an elliptic (oval) path. Earth's orbit has the shape of a slightly flattened circle.

WHY ARE THE PLANETS DIFFERENT TO EACH OTHER?

Although the nine planets in the Solar System were born at the same time, each one is different to another, in size and composition. The difference depends on their distance from the Sun and the effects caused by the gravity of the Sun at the moment of the birth of the Solar System. Mercury, Venus, Earth and Mars, the smallest and nearest the Sun, are 'earth' planets, formed of rock and metal. Jupiter, Saturn, Uranus and Neptune, the 'giants', much larger and further away, each have a nucleus of rock wrapped in thick layers of liquid and gas and circled by rings of dust, ice and stones. Pluto, the planet which is furthest from the Sun, is small and icy; some scientists believe that it is not a planet, but a comet.

Pluto

Neptune

Saturn

Uranus

● HOW WHY WHAT WHEN ●

Can asteroids fall to Earth?

Some asteroids pass very near to our planet and could even collide with it. However, there is a 'Space Survey Service' called the Spaceguard Foundation, which studies and prevents asteroids from coming too near the Earth. Thanks to the Foundation, it is possible to estimate the path of an asteroid in order to avoid an impact with Earth's surface.

Q·U·I·Z

1) **How many moons does Jupiter have?**

☐ 1 ☐ 16 ☐ none

2) **Which is the smallest planet?**

☐ Pluto ☐ Mercury ☐ Neptune

3) **Which of these planets has polar caps covered with ice?**

☐ Mars ☐ Jupiter ☐ Uranus

4) **Which of these planets has no satellites?**

☐ Venus ☐ Mercury ☐ Saturn

5) **Which planet spins in a clockwise direction?**

☐ Earth ☐ Neptune ☐ Venus

Answers
1) 16 2) Pluto 3) Mars 4) Mercury
5) Venus

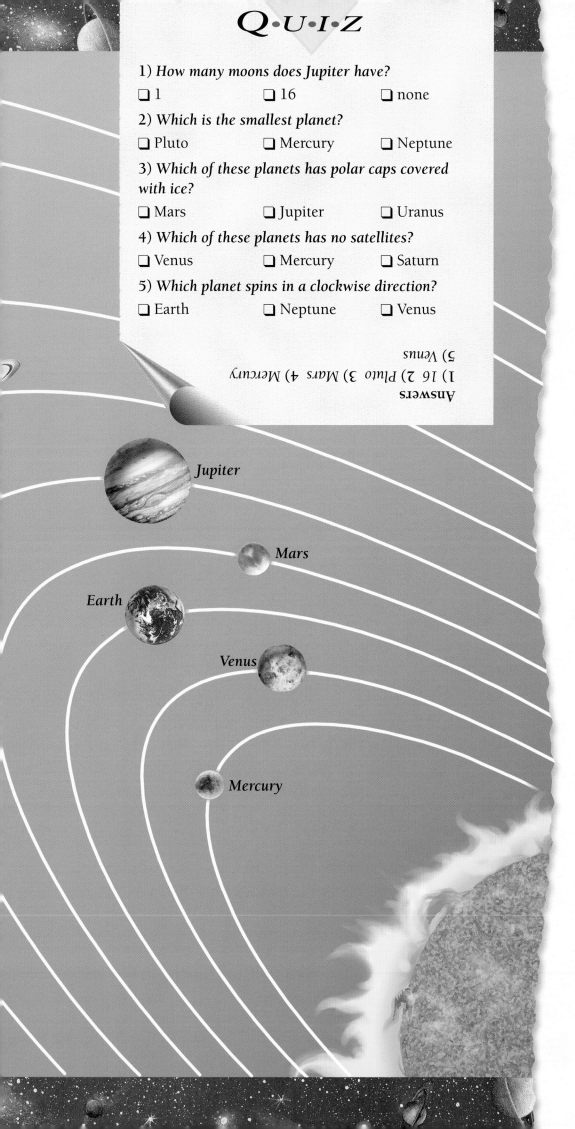

Jupiter

Mars

Earth

Venus

Mercury

PLANET FACTS

Jupiter is the largest planet in the Solar System – 1400 times the size of Earth.

Mercury is the planet nearest the Sun. It has the shortest orbit. To complete an orbit around the Sun it takes 88 Earth days.

Saturn is surrounded by many rings and spins at high speed on its axis; a day on Saturn would last only 10 hours. Saturn also has the most satellites, 18 in all.

Pluto is the smallest planet. It is also the coldest and the furthest from the Sun. Its orbit is noticeably inclined. Pluto takes more than 248 Earth years to complete one orbit around the Sun.

Venus is the planet which shines brightest. This is because it is surrounded by clouds, which reflect the light of the Sun. Spinning on its axis in a clockwise direction, Venus is very hot (480°C on its surface).

Mars at around 225 million kilometres from the Sun appears red, because of the oxydization (rusting) of the metal which covers it.

Uranus has its axis on which it rotates almost parallel to the path of its orbit around the Sun. So, it orbits sideways rather than upright around the Sun. It has 15 satellites.

Earth moves around the Sun at a speed of 29.8 kilometres per second. However, it is the only planet where there is water and where life has developed.

Neptune is distinguished by a bright blue colour. Its orbit around the Sun lasts more than 164 Earth years.

WHAT IS THE MOON?

The Moon is Earth's only natural satellite. It is a heavenly, lifeless body which orbits around our planet, whilst accompanying Earth on its journey around the Sun. It shines in the sky because it reflects light from the Sun. Its surface is composed of volcanic rock. The Moon has no atmosphere. That is why it has been hit repeatedly by meteorites which have made numerous craters in its surface.

THE AGE OF THE MOON
It is estimated that the Moon is about 4.5 billion years old. It is widely believed that the Moon was formed from a chip of the Earth which broke away when our planet was hit by a huge heavenly body before it solidified completely.

● HOW WHY WHAT WHEN ●

How is it that the Moon raises the level of the seas on Earth?

The rise and fall in the level of the sea – high and low tides – are due to the force of gravity of the Moon and to a lesser extent of the Sun. The Moon, like a huge magnet, attracts liquid masses in the Earth's hemisphere which is turned towards it, causing high tides. These happens twice each day, approximately every 12 hours and 25 minutes.

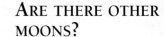

• On average, the Moon is 384,600km distant from the Earth. Because its orbit is elliptic, sometimes it is nearer, sometimes further from our planet.

• The Moon's diameter is a quarter of Earth's diameter – 3475.6km.

• The average temperature on the Moon goes from 100°C by day to minus 150°C by night.

• The hemisphere visible on the Moon is so vast that it could contain the whole of Europe.

ARE THERE OTHER MOONS?

Planets in the Solar System have different numbers of satellites or 'moons': Mars has 2; Jupiter 16; Saturn 18; Uranus 15; Neptune 8; Pluto 1.

Jupiter's largest moons are Ganymede, Callisto, Io and Europa, all discovered in 1610 by Galileo Galilei. Scientists think there may be water in a liquid state on Europa.

Mars' two moons are very small; 16km and 18km in diameter.

One of Saturn's moons, Titan, has an atmosphere of nitrogen and methane, which may suggest the presence of elementary forms of life.

Charon, Pluto's only known moon, is half the size of the planet.

THE SEAS ON THE MOON

When the Moon was first observed through telescopes, astronomers believed that the dark areas on the Moon's surface were seas. In fact, the 'seas' are vast plains of lava on the beds of gigantic meteorite craters.

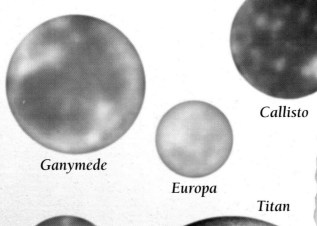

Ganymede

Callisto

Europa

Titan

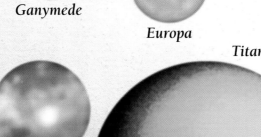

Io

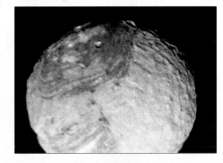

Miranda

Miranda, one of the moons of Uranus, has a very irregular surface, with plains, craters and canyons.

Triton, Neptune's largest moon, is the coldest place in the whole of the Solar System.

WHY DOES THE MOON NEVER LOOK THE SAME?

The Moon shines because it is illuminated by the Sun. It orbits around the Earth, whilst at the same time it accompanies Earth around the Sun. So, the position of the Moon in respect to our planet goes through different phases. The Moon is 'full' when it is directly opposite the Sun. It looks like a scythe when it receives light from the Sun sideways. It almost disappears when the Sun, behind it, only illuminates the side of the Moon which we never see. The phases during which the Moon is almost invisible is called the 'New Moon'. Between the New Moon and the 'Full Moon' (or 'waxing moon') there is the 'Crescent Moon'. Between the Full Moon and the New Moon is the Waning Moon.

• HOW WHY WHAT WHEN •

What is an Eclipse?

In the Solar System, planets can make shadows, one falling on another, according to their position in respect of the Sun. A solar eclipse happens when the Moon comes between the Earth and the Sun and projects a shadow on to the Sun which can hide the whole or a part. During a total eclipse, the sky darkens and only the corona of the Sun is visible, which we can see with special filters.

A lunar eclipse takes place when the Earth comes between the Moon and the Sun and the Moon passes through the shadow of the Earth. The Moon is not completely obscured, but is a pinkish colour. This is because some rays of the Sun still reach it, through the atmosphere of Earth.

THE "HUMP" OF THE MOON

There is an old saying - 'hump to the east of the Moon waning, hump to the west waxing'. This means that, to find out whether the Moon is in a waxing or waning phase, just look to see if the illuminated part has the 'hump' turned to the east or towards the west.

To understand the rotating movement of the Moon, we can use a puppet to represent the Earth, and a toy car to represent the Moon.

1) Put the puppet on a table. Take the toy car and push around the puppet. If you were in the place of the puppet, you would always see the same side of the toy car.

2) Now pick up the puppet and make the car go around it again. Watch the car, keeping your eyes at the height of the table. From this viewpoint, you can see it from all sides as it completes an entire orbit.

LUNAR PHASES

The cycle of lunar phases is called a 'lunar month' and lasts about 29 and a half days.

WHY DO WE ALWAYS SEE THE SAME SIDE OF THE MOON?

The Moon orbits in an anti-clockwise direction around the Earth, taking 27 days and 3 hours. Within the same interval of time it also completes a complete rotation on its own axis. That is why it is always the same side towards the Earth, making it seem that the Moon does not move. But we can try and understand the movements of the Moon as if we were looking at it from the outside.

The yellow part of the Moon indicates the side visible from Earth.

At the end of its orbit around the Earth, the Moon has completed one rotation on its own axis.

How many times has man landed on the Moon?

The US spacecraft Apollo 11 made a 'moon landing' possible. The first walk on the Moon was by Neil Armstrong and Edwin 'Buzz' Aldrin on 20 July 1969, after landing on the Moon's surface in the Lunar Module. A further five landings followed. The most recent was with Apollo 17, in December 1972. So far, twelve astronauts have explored the Moon.

The third astronaut

During the walk on the Moon by Neil Armstrong and Buzz Aldrin, a third astronaut, Michael Collins, waited in orbit around the Moon, in the Command Module.

● HOW WHY WHAT WHEN ●

Why do astronauts walk in 'bounces' on the surface of the Moon?

The weight of an object depends on the force of gravity in the place where that object is. On the Moon, the force of gravity is six times weaker than on Earth. So, the weight of a man on the Moon is one sixth that of a man on Earth. If on Earth he weighed 60kg, on the Moon he would weigh 10kg. Muscular force means he can easily overcome the weak attraction of the Moon's surface.

How was the spacecraft Apollo II constructed?

Apollo II had three modules; the Service Module (SM), the Command Module (CM) and the Lunar Module (LEM). Neil Armstrong and Buzz Aldrin landed in the LEM, using the 4-legged descent stage.

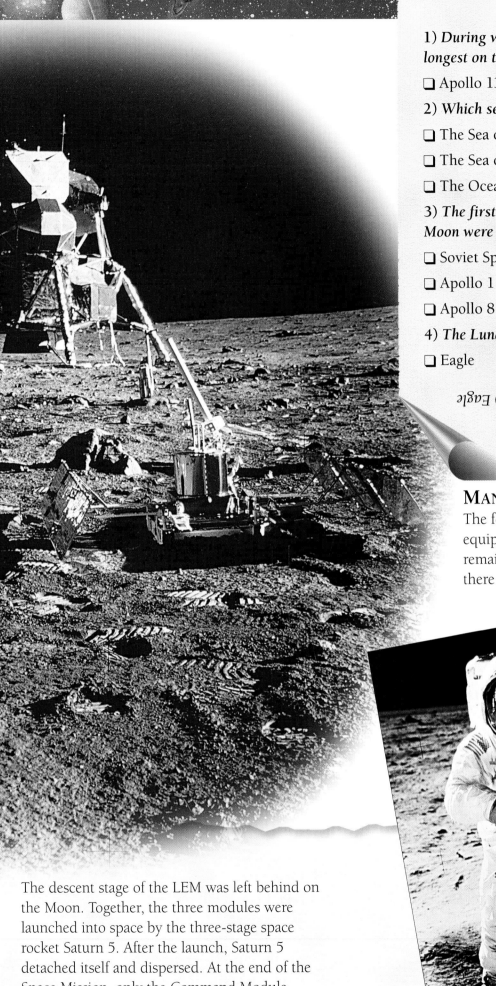

Q·U·I·Z

1) **During which mission did astronauts stay longest on the Moon?**

❏ Apollo 13   ❏ Apollo 17   ❏ Apollo 11

2) **Which sea did Apollo 11 land on?**

❏ The Sea of Tranquility

❏ The Sea of Crises

❏ The Ocean of Storms

3) **The first photographs of the hidden side of the Moon were taken by?**

❏ Soviet Space Probe Lunik in 1959

❏ Apollo 11 in 1969

❏ Apollo 8 in 1968

4) **The Lunar Module of Apollo was called?**

❏ Eagle   ❏ Columbia   ❏ Lunar Prospector

Answers

1) *Apollo 17, 22 hours and 5 minutes*
2) *In the Sea of Tranquility*
3) *In 1959, by the Space Probe Lunik* 4) *Eagle*

MAN'S FOOTPRINTS

The footprints of the astronauts and the equipment they used on the Moon will remain forever, because on the Moon there is neither wind nor rain.

The descent stage of the LEM was left behind on the Moon. Together, the three modules were launched into space by the three-stage space rocket Saturn 5. After the launch, Saturn 5 detached itself and dispersed. At the end of the Space Mission, only the Command Module returned to Earth, after separating from the others.

WHO MADE THE FIRST JOURNEY INTO SPACE?

The first success in overcoming the gravity of Earth and to leave Earth's atmosphere was by Sputnik I, a Russian artificial satellite. It was launched into space by powerful rockets in 1957.

The first space exploration by a human being was in 1961. Russian astronaut Yuri Gagarin was launched into space in the space capsule Vostok I and made a complete orbit around the Earth in 1 hour and 29 minutes at an estimated speed of 28000km per hour.

THE FIRST ORBIT AROUND THE EARTH

Sputnik I made an orbit around the Earth in 1 hour and 35 minutes, transmitting some very important data regarding features of Earth's atmosphere.

THE FIRST DOG IN SPACE

Before the space flight of Gagarin, Sputnik 2 was launched with a dog, Laika, on board, in order to study the reactions of a living animal to the conditions of a flight into space.

Sputnik 2

● HOW WHY WHAT WHEN ●

Who was the first woman in space?

The Russian Valentina Tereshkova was the first lady in space. In 1963, she journeyed for two days on board the spacecraft Vostok 6, completing 48 orbits around the Earth.

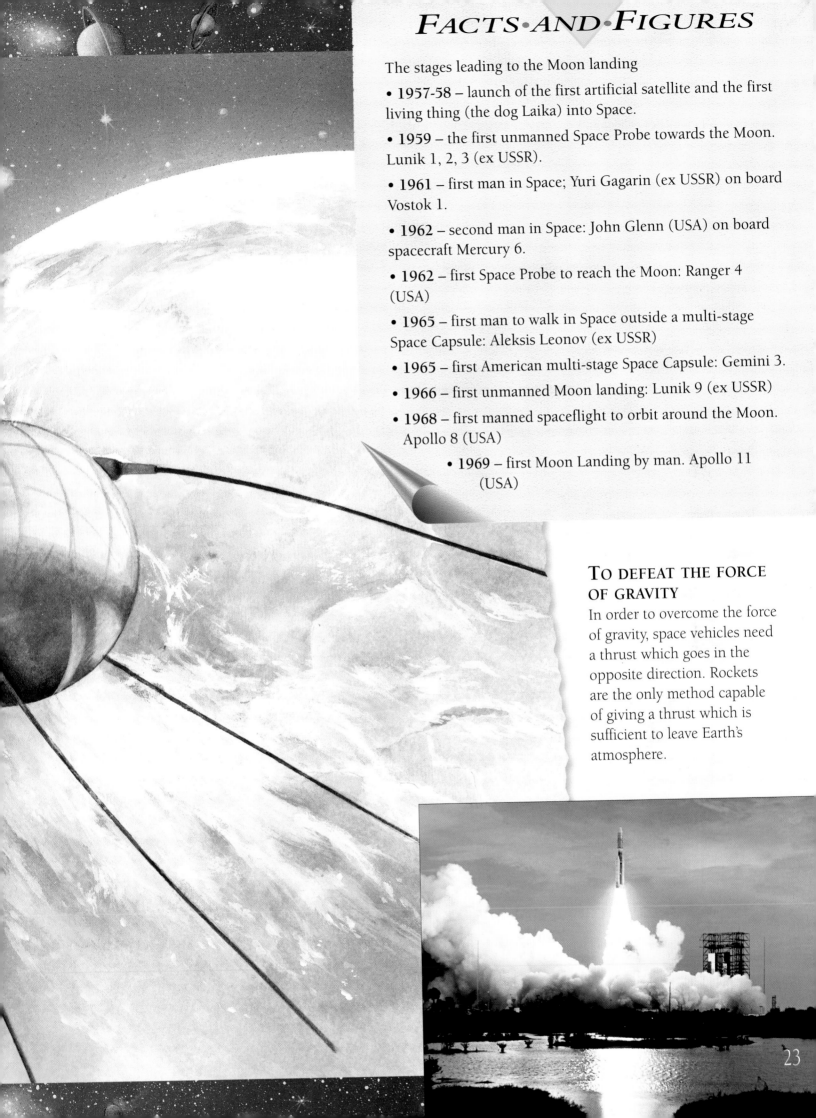

FACTS·AND·FIGURES

The stages leading to the Moon landing

- **1957-58** – launch of the first artificial satellite and the first living thing (the dog Laika) into Space.
- **1959** – the first unmanned Space Probe towards the Moon. Lunik 1, 2, 3 (ex USSR).
- **1961** – first man in Space; Yuri Gagarin (ex USSR) on board Vostok 1.
- **1962** – second man in Space: John Glenn (USA) on board spacecraft Mercury 6.
- **1962** – first Space Probe to reach the Moon: Ranger 4 (USA)
- **1965** – first man to walk in Space outside a multi-stage Space Capsule: Aleksis Leonov (ex USSR)
- **1965** – first American multi-stage Space Capsule: Gemini 3.
- **1966** – first unmanned Moon landing: Lunik 9 (ex USSR)
- **1968** – first manned spaceflight to orbit around the Moon. Apollo 8 (USA)
  - **1969** – first Moon Landing by man. Apollo 11 (USA)

TO DEFEAT THE FORCE OF GRAVITY

In order to overcome the force of gravity, space vehicles need a thrust which goes in the opposite direction. Rockets are the only method capable of giving a thrust which is sufficient to leave Earth's atmosphere.

WHICH PLANETS HAVE BEEN EXPLORED?

The only heavenly body which has been directly explored by man is the Moon. Other explorations have been made by Space Probes – without passengers, controlled from Earth, and capable of covering great distances and even reaching places far from the Solar System. The equipment on board these Space Probes give Control Stations data and images on the chemical and physical characteristics of the heavenly bodies. Some Space Probes have landed on surfaces of planets or satellites. The Russian Space Probe Venere has landed on Mars and in 1997 the Space Probe Pathfinder put the Robot Explorer Sojourner on Mars.

Other Space Probes have transmitted detailed data and images of all planets in the Solar System.

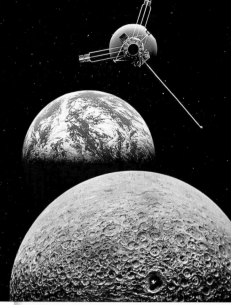

Pioneer 10

WHAT IS GRAVITATIONAL SLING-SHOT?

A Space Probe cannot carry large quantites of fuel. So, instead of using engines to change direction or to accelerate, the Probe is directed nearer a planet. The force of gravity from this planet can then control the curved path of the Probe and its speed. This operation is called 'gravitational sling-shot'.

● HOW WHY WHAT WHEN ●

Can a Space Probe leave the Solar System

The US Space Probe Pioneer 10 was launched in 1972. After having gone beyond the orbit of Neptune, it is now directed towards Proxima Centurai, towards the edge of the Solar System. Proxima Centurai is the star nearest to us. Pioneer 10 will reach it in about 26,000 years. Pioneer 10 was overtaken in 1998 by the Space Probe Voyager 1, after having gone near Saturn. Voyager 1 is now the Space Probe furthest from Earth – at a distance of 0.4 billion kilometres!

Is it possible to live on the Moon?

Living on the Moon would mean that we could use the resources of its sub-surface, rich in metals, to build scientific laboratories, launch-bases and space observatories. The project to populate the Moon may provide solutions to enable the growth of food, electrical energy to provide protection from solar radiation and extremes of temperature and to remedy the lack of gravity. But the biggest problem will be the total lack of water. However, in 1996, the US Lunar Space Probe Clementine sent back information that both poles of the Moon are covered with a great mass of water in its solid state, confirmed two years later by the US Lunar Robot Prospector. This discovery has re-opened the door to the possibility of a lunar city.

What will a lunar city be like?

It will have solar panels for the production of electrical energy, laboratories, shops, and areas for the landing and take-off of space vehicles. One of the projects forecast for the Lunar City (Escargot City 2050) are houses and buildings similar to the shells of snails. (*Escargot* is French for snail.)

A Journey into Space

The special spacesuit which astronauts wear for their 'walks in space' enable them to breathe oxygen, to overcome the extremely cold temperatures of Outer Space and also to carry out, in the absence of gravity, repairs to the spacecraft or to the space base. To protect the astronaut from cold the spacesuit inside is criss-crossed with little tubes containing hot liquid, like little radiators to give warmth to the smallest finger. When necessary, the astronaut can also put on the spacesuit inside the spacecraft to refresh himself with oxygen. On the front of the spacesuit is the housing for all tools, each with a retractable thread so that nothing floats off into space. The helmet is fixed to the spacesuit and inside the astronaut can turn his head freely. The visor is mirrored, to protect the eyes from solar radiation.

When the astronaut has to work on the remote-control arms, he has to stay firmly in a particular place. So, he puts his feet into special boots fixed to the walls.

- The spacesuit worn for 'walks in spac weighs 47kg.
- The helmet weighs 4kg.
- There are buttons for the propulsion the MMU (Manoeuvre Movement Unit)
- The remote-controlled robot arm which is controlled from inside the Shuttle can launch and retrieve satellite in space. It can also carry out repairs. It is divided into three parts and can be moved in six directions. Each arm is 16.8m long.
- The EMU (Extra-vehicular Mobility Unit) weighs 68kg an contains batteries, cooling systems and oxygen.

How does an astronaut move in space?

Thanks to the MMU the astronaut can move on a sort of flying armchair. This has push-buttons on the arms to manoeuvre the movement.

The EMU comes fixed to the back and is equipped with a little rocket which the astronaut uses to move.

HOW IS A SPACECRAFT SET OUT?

The 1970 Space Mission was carried out using non-reusable vehicles, which were mostly destroyed. The Space Shuttle vehicles have been designed to use many times and have been designed to transport and to put into orbit artificial satellites or to transport laboratories and space stations.

The Shuttle comprises a vehicle similar to an aeroplane, the Orbiter, which enters in orbit and then returns to Earth by two outer recoverable rockets, called 'boosters', and by one giant external fuel tank. The Shuttle is equipped with manoeuvrable motors to control the flight both in orbit and the return.

FACTS·AND·FIGURES

• The hold of the Space Shuttle is 18m long and 4m wide.
• The Shuttle can carry in orbit 29 tonnes of cargo and bring back 15 tonnes to Earth.
• In 1986 the Space Shuttle Challenger on its tenth flight exploded soon after its launch, killing all seven members of the crew; launches were suspended for two years after.
• In 1988 the ex Soviet Union launched their first unmanned space shuttle, Buran.

THE PHASES OF FLIGHT

1) Launch is vertical, pushed up by the principal motors and booster rockets.

2) At a height of around 50km, the booster drops off and falls into the ocean.

3) At 100km, the external fuel tank drops off and disintegrates in the atmosphere.

4) With the aid of the manoeuvre motor, the spacecraft goes into orbit and reaches maximum speed.

5) To come back, the spacecraft positions itself in the opposite direction and fires the motors to move out of orbit.

6) At re-entry into the atmosphere, the spacecraft overheats by friction with the air and at some points reaches about 1500°C.

7) Finally the Shuttle lands in a gliding flight and comes down with the aid of a parachute.

Is it possible to live in space?

For some years, the USA, Russia, Europe, Canada and Japan have been working on the construction of the largest Space Station ever realized. It is hoped that this will come into use some time during the first years of the 21st Century. Inside there will be six laboratories, in which scientists from all over the world will work together. Both the equipment and the scientists will undergo a rigorous training programme, under the constant control of doctors during their time in space, which could last more than three or four months. As before, the main challenge to human beings will be to adapt themselves to the lack of gravity, being able to work, to wash, to eat and to sleep in Space in the same way as they do on Earth.

● HOW WHY WHAT WHEN ●

What other space stations have been launched in space?

The first Russian Space Station Salyut ('Salute') 1 was put into orbit in 1971. The last was Salyut 7 in 1982.
Skylab was launched in 1973 by the USA. The last crew returned to Earth in 1974. In 1979, the Station disintegrated into the atmosphere.
The Russian Space Station Mir was in service from 1986 to 1997.

THE BODY IN SPACE

Tests and studies on astronauts have shown that, during space missions, the muscles become weakened and the bones lose calcium.

HOW DO PEOPLE LIVE IN A SPACE STATION?

Inside the Space Station all is arranged to overcome the lack of gravity. In the shower-rooms, the water is sucked up from the floor to avoid it flying away! In the laboratories, there are hooks to keep boots firmly fixed, so that scientists can

28

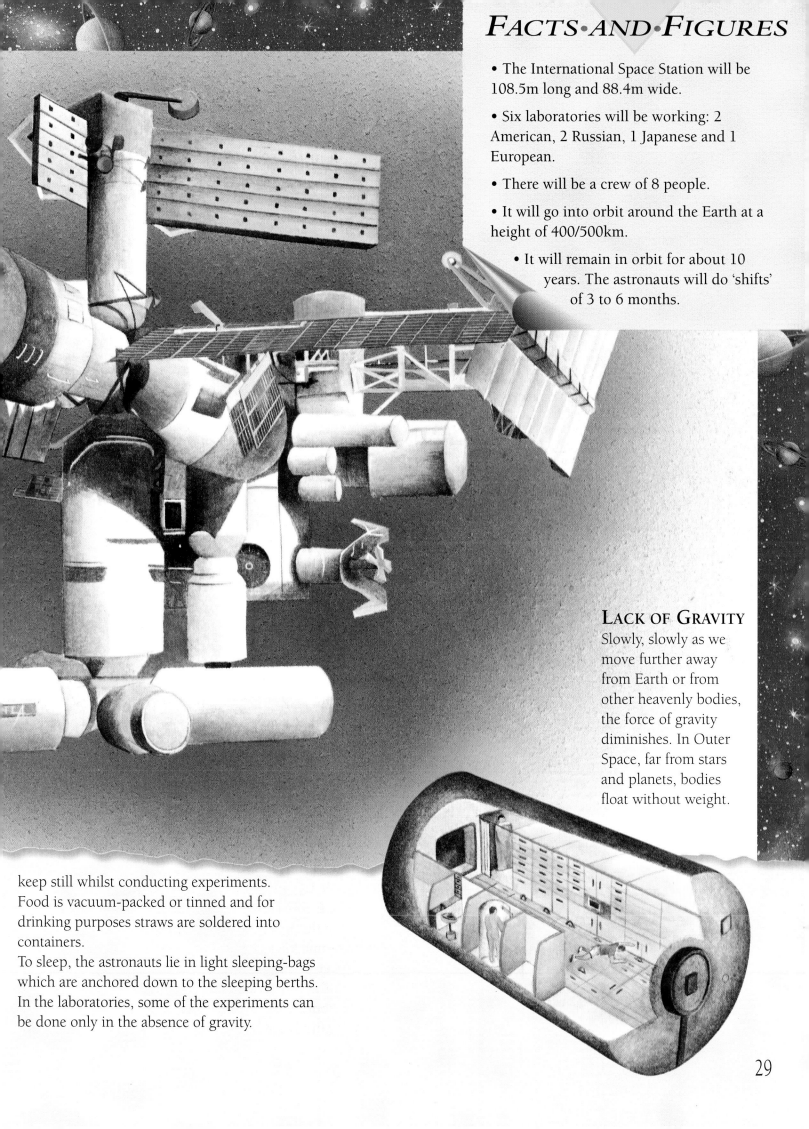

FACTS·AND·FIGURES

- The International Space Station will be 108.5m long and 88.4m wide.

- Six laboratories will be working: 2 American, 2 Russian, 1 Japanese and 1 European.

- There will be a crew of 8 people.

- It will go into orbit around the Earth at a height of 400/500km.

- It will remain in orbit for about 10 years. The astronauts will do 'shifts' of 3 to 6 months.

LACK OF GRAVITY

Slowly, slowly as we move further away from Earth or from other heavenly bodies, the force of gravity diminishes. In Outer Space, far from stars and planets, bodies float without weight.

keep still whilst conducting experiments. Food is vacuum-packed or tinned and for drinking purposes straws are soldered into containers.

To sleep, the astronauts lie in light sleeping-bags which are anchored down to the sleeping berths. In the laboratories, some of the experiments can be done only in the absence of gravity.

WHAT DOES AN ARTIFICIAL SATELLITE DO?

The sky above us is full of numerous artificial satellites, put into orbit around the Earth for many purposes – to receive and transmit television and telephonic signals, to relay data on weather conditions, to observe regions of the planet for military, industrial and agricultural purposes, furnishing data for study on Earth about pollution, mapping the stars and to keep track of the navigation of ships and aircraft. Artificial satellites are often equipped with solar panels which transform the rays of the Sun into an energy which can be used in their work.

- The first artificial satellite put into orbi was the Soviet Sputnik 1 (1957).

- The first American artificial satellite wa Explorer 1 (1958).

- The first weather satellite was Tiros 1 (1960, USA).

- The first telecommunication satellite w Syncom 2 (1963, USA).

- The first satellite around Mars was Mariner 9 (1971, USA)

HOW DO ARTIFICIAL SATELLITES REMAIN IN ORBIT?

When an object is launched i the air, it makes a curved trai To prevent space vehicles fall back to Earth, they need rockets to give them a speed at least 27000km per hour. In this way, the vehicle overcom the force of gravity, finishes it launching stage and enters in orbit around the earth, alway travelling at the same distanc just like natural satellites.

THE DEVELOPMENT OF OUR 'HIGH TECH' AGE

10 July 1962 The USA launch **Telstar 1**. This was the first artificial satellite to transmit live television signals across the Atlantic Ocean, from the USA to Europe. Telstar 1 was also the first to transmit a live telephone conversation, proving that 'instant' transatlantic communication was possible.

26 July 1963 The first communications satellite **Syncom 2** is launched by the USA. Now, a caller in the UK, would be able to dial the telephone number of a person in the USA and be connected immediately. Before then, a caller needed to contact the local telephone exchange and ask a telephone operator to book the call. Then came a lengthy wait, often for hours, until the connection was made and the person being called came on the line.

6 April 1965 The **'Early Bird' satellite** (now more widely known as **Intelstat 1**) was launched by the USA. This was the first commercial communications satellite, providing a more powerful telecommunications link between the United States and Europe. Now, the 'high tech' age was really beginning!

1970 – 1980 The USA launch more **Intelstat** satellites. By the end of the 1980, more than 20 countries launch artificial satellites for their own telecommunication purposes. More than two thirds of all international telephone calls are transmitted through satellite channels.

1980 – 1990 Satellite communications lead to the development of high-powered optical fibre networks which make telecommunication even quicker. We see the first FAX machines, faster communication via radio, television and computer.

From 1990 The use of artificial satellites leads to a boom in the use of mobile telephones. Communication via computerized links becomes even faster. The use of the Internet, the world wide web and correspondence by email rapidly becomes widespread. 'Video conferences' and 'video discussions' take the place of lengthy and expensive journeys for business and pleasure.

INDEX